© Rod Campbell 1988
First published 1988 by
Campbell Blackie Books
7 Leicester Place · London WC2H 7BP
All rights reserved

ISBN 1 85292 014 9

Printed in Singapore

Little Learners

colours

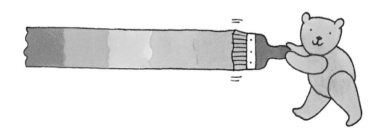

Rod Campbell

CAMPBELL BLACKIE BOOKS

red

a red tomato
juicy and round

orange

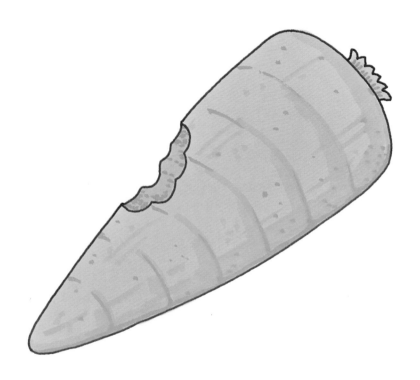

an orange carrot
that grows in the ground

yellow

a yellow chick
pecking for food

green

a green frog
who's in a bad mood

blue

a blue sky
with no clouds to be seen

purple

a purple plum
that started off green!

brown

a brown puppy
wagging his tail

pink

a pink flower
with petals so pale

white

a white polar bear
who thinks swimming is fun

grey

a grey elephant
who loves the hot sun

black

a black cat
who would like to know...

what is the colour of these things below?

biscuit

beads

mug

spoon

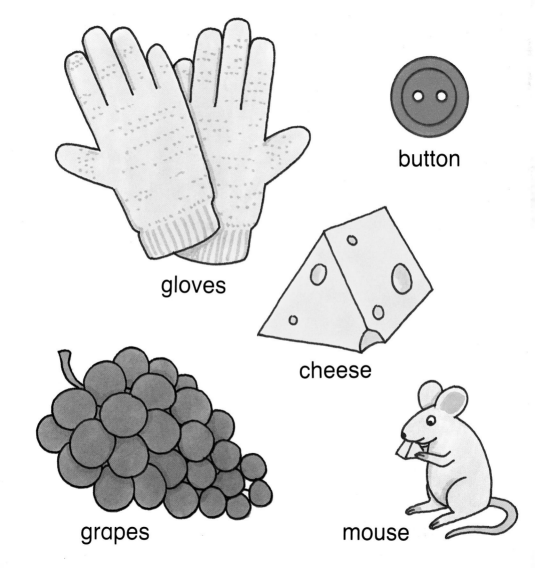

gloves

button

cheese

grapes

mouse